When a Man Loves a Woman

14 Tips
From God's Word
To Having an Enriched
And
Better Marriage

DR. DAVID SCOTT

PURPLE CHAIR BOOKS
AND EDUCATIONAL PRODUCTS, LLC.

PCB

Published by Purple Chair Books and Educational Products, LLC
First Printing, 2020
Copyright © Dr. David Scott, 2021
Scott, David 1969-

When a Man Loves a Woman
14 Tips
From God's Word
To Having an Enriched
And
Better Marriage
By Dr. David Scott

ISBN: 978-1-953671-02-8

Christian Life/ Spiritual 1.Title
Printed in the United States of America
Set in Adobe Garamond Pro

Interior Designed by Sarco Press

Publisher's Note

THIS PUBLICATION AIMS to offer hope, encouragement and a Christian perspective. This book is sold with the understanding that the publisher or author is not engaged in rendering psychological, therapeutic or other professional services. If corrective, psychological counseling or additional expert help is required, a competent professional person's services should be sought.

Without limiting the rights under copyright reserved above, part of this publication may be reproduced, stored or introduced into a retrieval system or transmitted, in any form or by any means (electronic, mechanical, photocopying, recording or otherwise), without the prior written permission of both the copyright owner and the above publisher of this book.

Contents

Publisher's Note iii
Dedication vii
Acknowledgment ix
Introduction xi
Tip #1: Appreciate and Value your Wife 1
Tip #2: Stop Thinking and Acting like a Loner 11
Tip #3: Remain Faithful 19
Tip #4: Love and Cherish the Gift God gave you 29
Tip #5: Honor God/ Love her as she is 37
Tip #6: Treasure and Never Mistreat Her 47
Tip #7: Prize and Respect Her 55
Tip #8: Care and Protect Her 63
Tip #9: Resist Sexual Temptation 73
Tip #10: Love and be willing to Sacrifice 83
Tip #11: Love Unselfishly 93
Tip #12: Let Love Command Respect 101
Tip #13: Practice Gentleness 109
Tip #14: Communication and Understanding is Key 119
Final Thoughts 129

Dedication

THIS BOOK IS dedicated to the Godly men striving with all diligence to honor and fulfill their duties and obligations in the coveted and ordained role of husband. It is not always an easy, joyous or delightful task. However, you should be commended for your tenaciousness, grit and determination. Far too may fail, quit or lack the courage to enter the arena.

Acknowledgment

THANK YOU TO my number one fan, my companion, partner, inspiration and cheerleader. You are the light of my days, thoughts of my nights and the smile on my face. I cannot thank you enough for your innumerable prayers, words of encouragement, and unwavering support. I could not ask for a more fitting and appropriate first lady and bride. Thank you, TT, for always being here or there with me. You are my most prized treasure.

Introduction

MARRIAGE IS A beautiful union to be enjoyed between a man and woman. Although some might challenge this idea, this institution's Creator and Framer is the ultimate authority and final say. From the beginning of creation, He made clear His instructions, purpose and reasoning. As men and women choose to formulate their own opinions, ideas and justifications for rebellion, it does not negate His authority. God created the woman for the man, giving the man a special charge and obligation. He has not changed or deviated from His original plan and intention. Those that profess to be followers of Christ and believers in His word must either adhere to it or abandon it altogether. To please God is an all or nothing proposition. Jesus said to those that professed belief in Him in John 8:31, "You are truly my disciples if you remain faithful to my teachings." We are only His and we please the Father when we are obedient, no matter the cost or sacrifice.

God created marriage for man and woman to have fellowship together and with Him. In this union, God has promised to bless them, visit and commune with them in the relationship. Any partnership between man and woman functioning outside of

God's mandates is fraudulent and counterfeit. Living as husband and wife is not marriage. Merely living together and calling it marriage is not what God intended. God designed marriage to be a full, recognized, and displayed union and commitment to the world. Living together without the recognized union and ritual of marriage is a shame and a forgery of the authentic. Such relationships will not receive the blessing and grace of God. In such unions, there can never be genuine and authentic joy, security and peace. The blessing and sanction of God can only be found in the legal and authorized union of marriage. God honors obedience. If a man and woman want the best God has for them, they must adhere and follow His perfect plan. He will neither bend nor compromise. He is the Eternal God that does not change.

Statistics shows that in 2016, the number of Americans living with an unmarried partner, cohabitating or "shacking up" reached 18 million, indicating increased numbers from 2007. Although roughly half are younger than 35, sadly, these numbers are rapidly increasing among adults ages 50 and older. God is not pleased. He will not change or lower his standard. It is His will and expectation that His creation obeys their Creator. It is not His desire that men and women willingly choose experiences beneath his best.

A 2019 Pew Research Center report stated that large majorities of Generation Zers, Millennials, Generation Xers and Baby Boomers say couples living without being married does not make a difference for our society. This report goes on to say that while 54% in the Silent Generation says cohabitation does not make a difference in society, about four in ten (41%) acknowledge it is not a good thing. The opinions of man in apparent defiance to God's law and standards cannot be considered right. As the Creator, it is reasonable and logical that His instructions would serve best. The designer or manufacturer of most things offers or provides instructions for its best function. Marriage also comes with instructions from the Creator. The results of violating His guidance are evident in statistical data. Research informs that 50% of all marriages in America end in divorce. However, it points out specifically 41% of all first marriages, 60% of all second marriages and 73% of all third; America has the sixth highest divorce rate globally.

The most significant and commonly reported factors contributing to divorce are a lack of commitment, infidelity, communication, abuse, arguing and emotional conflict. However, the single most significant and recurring factor is money, including negligence, lack and the inequity of shared resources. These might seem like acceptable reasons to divorce; however, God is not pleased. It is not His will that men and women break the bonds of their union. Marriage is a holy and sacred institution. Where is the love so enthusiastically professed? Where is the commitment vowed? Where is the sacrifice owed to the other? No matter the reason, God hates divorce. Divorce is Satan's work of divisiveness and destruction of what God intended for his crown jewel of creation.

As our divine and gracious Father, God always knows best, He created the beautiful union of marriage so men and women might become complete, whole as one. As God made two from one, in marriage's sanctity, he again makes one of two. There are no mistakes in His plans. Whatever He does is right—the architect of the universe created marriage. No government, delegation, committee or group envisioned something so magnificent. No organization or think-tank developed it. The institution of marriage was irrefutably conceived in the unsearchable mind of the holy God. The American Christian Missionary, John C. Broger stated, "God intends and expects marriage to be a lifetime commitment between a man and a woman, based on the principles of biblical love. The relationship between Jesus Christ and His Church is the supreme example of the committed love that a husband and wife are to follow in their relationship with each other." Speaking about the beauty of marriage, the great Protestant Reforming Martin Luther said, "There is no more lovely, friendly or charming relationship, communion or company, than a good marriage." Lastly, to husbands, the Quaker and founder of the Pennsylvania colony said, "In marriage do thou wise: prefer the person before money, virtue before beauty, the mind before the body; then thou hast a wife, a friend, a companion, a second self."

When a Man Loves a Woman

14 Tips
From God's Word
To Having an Enriched
And
Better Marriage

Tip #1

Appreciate and value the wife God has entrusted to you. To have a partner is a privilege, not a right!

Genesis 2:18 "Then the LORD God said, "It is not good for the man to be alone. I will make a helper who is just right for him."

From a tender age, men are taught to be strong, brave, tough, courageous and even when challenged, invincible. As small, impressionable little boys, instead of being allowed to develop as we might, it is pressed upon us that we are little men. We do our best not to or show weakness. We suck it up and drive on no matter the circumstance or situation, learning quite early on that boys endure, suffer and carry the full brunt of the load. It is ingrained in us as soon we can comprehend that we are expected to do what men do; we tend to like trucks, cars, sports and guns, the usual manly stuff, as well as support and participate in masculine activities, while seldom communicating our hurts and pains. We learn early on that real men do not get hurt, or at least they never show it. We are Men!

Far too often, the aspiration to satisfy this predetermined idea surrounding manhood leads to many harmful and unnecessary experiences. Because the world we live in has predetermined what defines a man, we traverse life compelled to follow, measure up and adhere fully and entirely to this definition. We draw images of masculinity from what we view on television and media, as well as from models around us. These images, in most cases, are a far distance from what God intended. Media and music would have us believe the culture of being single, becoming a player and hooking up are endlessly pleasing and satisfying. However, this is untrue and damaging leading us down paths we are not meant to follow. Although pleasures may be enjoyable for a season, trying to satisfy the world's definition of masculinity and manliness takes more from us than we intend to give. Sleeping with different women, no matter how beautiful, ultimately destroys us physically draining our sexual ability, endurance and stamina and spiritually. It robs us of the ability to form real connections, authentic passion and the ability to share genuine intimacy.

The world's ideas of a man are far from God's plan. We were never intended to go through life trying to figure it out, bumbling, damaging and destroying others' lives along the way. Our manhood was never to be determined by numbers or notches on our belts. We have not achieved great conquests. We have damaged and bruised the hearts, minds and souls of countless daughters, sisters and future mothers along this brief life's journey. We were never meant to live any way we 'choose and deem' acceptable. God has always been and is fully aware of our needs, as well as what compliments us best.

The scriptures speak of God's profound wisdom and concern regarding man. The writer tells us in Genesis 2:18 that God looked around and considered the works of his great power; He recognized man though perfect, was still lacking and needed something more, and said, "It is not good that man should be alone; I will make him a helper fit for him." God created a helper, perfect in association and comparison for the man he created. Nothing in all creation compliments the man except his counterpart, the woman. God understood that man needed a partner, someone to help, support and encourage him through this life. A man needs someone to help him accomplish goals and objectives. He

Tip #1

benefits from having someone to share ideas, plans and dreams. A man needs a companion to share life's highs and lows and offer a distinctly different perspective, someone to give him balance, insight and ulterior consideration.

A man was never meant to be alone; however, he was also never permitted to have a plethora of women. From the beginning, the Creator joined one man to one woman. Because we were never intended to journey and travel life alone, God created a special, unique and perfect partner for each of us. She is all and everything we need. She was designed to be our strength where we are weak, soft where we are unbending, and support when we are falling. She is everything we fail to recognize we need. God has made her be our perfect fit, as a piece to a jigsaw puzzle.

It is not her job to find us. On the contrary, it is the man's quest to discover her. Each of us is made and wired distinctly, having our specific likes and dislikes. We are each equipped with our known unique quirks. Amazingly, in His matchless grace and kindness, God created and designed a perfect fit for each of our lives. When we find and discover them, we should thank God for his divine love and favor.

"Marriage is a beautiful fellowship and precious gift. It is God's reflection and design, created between a man and a woman."

-Dr. David Scott
Pastor/Educator

Thoughts and Reflections

Areas of Improvement

1. _____

_____

_____

2. _____

_____

_____

3. _____

_____

_____

Prayer for Strength and Bonding

Father, nothing is impossible or difficult for you. I am grateful that you specialize in hard cases. You delight in the opportunity to prove your power. God, I pray that you would join and unite those that have been courageous enough to choose, in a fallen world, to live in holy matrimony, honoring each other and you as the Creator of this perfect design. Lord, help this husband to understand his role, duty and obligation. Help him to respect, appreciate and value the privilege you have allowed. God, help him keep his eyes locked and steadied on you, the chief example and model provider, protector, lover and friend. Sovereign King, give him wisdom when he is lacking, strength when he is weak and courage when it is easiest to surrender. Help him in every way, and every situation; increase respect, admiration and love for the gift you have given him, recognizing it is not right that any man should be alone, Amen.

Tip #2

Stop thinking and acting like a loner. God has given you a helper and companion. Two united are better than one!

Genesis 2:24 "This explains why a man leaves his father and mother and is joined to his wife, and the two are united into one."

As men, we have an obligation and responsibility to the partners and wives that God has been so gracious and kind to give us. If we have been blessed to be given a wife and partner, then we have a clearly defined and specific role. Our role is to be a husband. We are expected to get up, leave our parents' home and secure a place for our partner. It is our responsibility to provide a place, home or dwelling where she can be the woman of the house. You are the husband (house-band), the one chosen and designated to hold the house and family together.

I know many of us have been taught and led to believe that nobody can ever take our mother's place. Though true, when you take on the responsibility, duty and obligation of caring for a wife, she becomes the new priority in our lives. Our mothers will always hold a dear and unique place in our hearts, but our wives are the gift that God has given and entrusted to us. Our mothers have a distinct and memorable role as a parent. Our wives have a more significant and God-ordained role and function as a partner, co-regent, confidante and life companion. When mother and father are gone, it is the wife that will be there. When we are sick, tired, up, down, rich or poor, our wives are expected to help us through all situations and circumstances. Likewise, we are expected to be by her side as well.

Above all else, a man is supposed to hold to his wife. He is expected to cling to her, hold her close, value and recognize her for the treasure she is and will be in his life. A man is expected to love his wife, not in word only, but in the way he treats her. She is intended to be everything to him. He is to share with her in all things. She is to be viewed with pride, admiration, respect and appreciation. As a married couple, the man and the woman are intended to join in unity in every aspect. The two partners are expected to be so joined and connected that they share and complement each other in all things. Their love for each other is intended to be so strong, pure, authentic and unhindered though they are two separate persons; they are meant to be so intentional in their love for each other that it appears as if they are one. The two are expected to become one in purpose, objective, plans and direction for the life they will share for the rest of their lives.

"A good marriage is the union of two people that recognize they are best together."

-Dr. David Scott
Pastor/Educator

Thoughts and Reflections

Areas of Improvement

1. _____

_____

_____

2. _____

_____

_____

3. _____

_____

_____

Prayer for Unity and Togetherness

Father, I pray for this union. I pray for the power of your spirit to move, reign and have complete control in every area. I pray that you would be all and only what you can be. God, I ask that you be the dominant source of strength, comfort and consolation in this union. Bring together the minds and hearts of these two that you have joined by your great and divine wisdom. Nothing is impossible with you. You can do and accomplish what no other can. You alone can mend the broken, heal undeclared hurt and fortify all weakness. Great and Eternal God, bind these two as one. Unite them in spirit, love and purpose. Please help them to recognize the gift you have extended and provided each in the other. Lord, teach them the beauty of your way and help them see that you are the author, finisher and Creator of all things beautiful. Show and demonstrate to them how precious they are in your sight; they are capable, but stronger together. Help them strive with diligence, commitment and purpose to serve you and accomplish your perfect will for their lives by loving each other as they love themselves, Amen.

Tip #3

Remain faithful to your covenant partner. Under no circumstance should you violate your marriage vow!

Exodus 20:14 "You must not commit adultery."

IT IS NOT a suggestion, but the will and command of God that we do not commit adultery. No matter the situation or circumstance, it is God's will that we remain faithful and loyal to our partners. This commandment is for both husbands and wives. However, with the wealth of temptations and readily available opportunities with Social Media and technology advancement, it is easier now than ever before to hookup and cheat; all we need do is swipe left. Also, in a world where ethics and morality are on the decline in society today, finding somebody with no strings attached, or so it seems, is so easy to do. Perceived free sex is only a text, click or swipe away. However, physical pleasure, cheap intimacy and illegitimate sex outside of the marital union are never free. There is always a cost. Somebody and, often, all parties pay, now or later. The old adage is still true. You might get by, but you will not getaway. Sex outside the lawful bonds of Marriage always costs. Somebody suffers emotionally, physically, psychologically and spiritually. Nobody ever gets away clean.

After we say the words "I DO," God's divine plan is that the only woman we ever engage in the intimate act with is our lawful wife. Any relationship of a physical nature outside of Marriage is illegitimate and a violation of God's will. It will not be blessed.

It will not prosper. We will not find happiness, fulfillment or contentment in it, no matter how good it feels momentary. The pleasures of sin are enjoyable for a season. However, they will ultimately only bring us sadness. We are commanded not to violate our Marriage vows to love and hold only her for the rest of our lives. We must not break that covenant promise, no matter how hard and challenging it might be at times. We have a friend that stands with us; He is closer than a brother. When we are weak, struggling and in trouble, we can ask God to help us. The scripture is clear in Hebrews 4:14-16, "Since we have a great High Priest who has entered heaven, Jesus, the Son of God, let us hold firmly to what we believe. This High Priest of ours understands our weaknesses, for he faced all of the same tests we do, yet he did not sin. So let us come boldly to the throne of our gracious God. There, we will receive his mercy and find grace to help us when we need it most."

We have no legitimate excuse to cheat. Women can be difficult, challenging and, at times, unbearable. However, God has commanded us to remain faithful. No relationship outside our own will ever give us happiness. No matter how attractive, alluring, and appealing she might be, no woman can satisfy our true desires like the one God has so graciously provided. In his commandment, God demonstrates great love and compassion for us. He tells us not to commit adultery for our benefit. As a loving father, he attempts to guard us against the sadness, heartaches and pain associated with illegitimate sex. When God commands us not to commit the act of adultery, it is not to harm or deny us anything. Whatever God does is for our benefit. God is perfect in his doings and dealings. He does all things wonderful. When God denies, it is to deliver.

God is gracious whatever he does is to keep us from unnecessary hurt and sadness. He forbids us from having sex outside

Tip #3

of Marriage because of the curse, heartache, sadness and pain it brings to all involved. He is a loving father. God will never withhold any good thing from us. Scriptures tell us that God desires that we prosper, thrive and have success in all things. If adultery were in our best interest, he would permit it. Since the act of adultery under any circumstance does not help us in any way, God must and will always forbid it.

"A good husband will run in the opposite direction of anything that might distract him or cause him to hurt the love of his life."

-Dr. David Scott
Pastor/Educator

Thoughts and Reflections

Areas of Improvement

1. _____

_____

_____

2. _____

_____

_____

3. _____

_____

_____

Prayer for Faithfulness and Commitment

Oh God, I pray that you would show yourself strong. I ask O Lord that you would keep this man and woman joined in the marital union from the Evil one's influences and seductive powers. God, I pray that you wrap your massive and powerful arms around them and hold them tightly in your warm and divine embrace. I pray that you shield their minds and imaginations from every temptation and desire of sexual deviation and impurity. Dear Lord, I ask that you keep this man's mind on you and his affections on the wife of his choosing. I ask O God that you keep him in hard times. Guide him through every struggle and difficult trial. Where he is weak, make him strong. When the Tempter comes, provide a way for his escape. I ask you to be a solid rock to stand on, a hiding place to weather the storm and a shield against the attacks of Satan. I know you can do all things, and all things you do are well. So, I ask all these things by faith. Amen.

Tip #4

Love and cherish the wife God chose and gave you. Give her all of yourself and no one else. Trust Him. He does not make mistakes!

Proverbs 5:15 "Drink water from your own well—share your love only with your wife."

As husbands, God challenges us to evaluate and find joy and contentment with what we have. We are to drink from our well, the beautiful fountain God has made our own. There is a benefit in having someone to come home to after a long, tiring and challenging day. How blessed we are to have abandoned the game. No more days and nights of imaginative lies, perpetrations, games of deceit, playing the chameleon, wasting time, money and energies. God has blessed us with a partner, giving us someone in whom we can invest. He has given us a partner with whom we can build and achieve.

If we do the work to cultivate a loving, nurturing and supportive relationship, we can always get what we need from our partners. Like a financial institution that holds secure our monetary resources, we can readily make necessary withdrawals if we have made frequent and robust deposits. In most scenarios, we can withdraw more than we have put in. Our relationships are no different. If we make regular, necessary and deliberate deposits into our companion's heart, soul and spirit, we can always draw deeply from her well.

God tells us to drink from our cisterns. It is there we should find the quench for our thirst and refreshment. We have no reason or need to be concerned or involved with another man's wife, companion and partner, no matter how appealing. It is reasonable to admire some aspects of another woman. However, it must never go beyond admiration. We must never allow it to turn into desire, obsession or lust. All our passions, yearnings and desires belong to our wives. If God has granted us the privilege of being a husband, our wives should to lifted in the highest esteem. We are to treat her well, making her feel appreciated. We must work diligently to make her realize she is wanted and needed. Our obligation and responsibility are to gently teach her how to compliment us, meeting our needs best. We do not have the right to mistreat her for any perceived shortcomings. It is the husband's responsibility with love, tenderness and respect to show her how to be a helper and make us content and happy with her.

A wife can only become exceptional and outstanding if she is developed and encouraged to be. Let her be the single and complete source of your satisfaction. She does not know how to be what you need unless you take the time and initiative to cultivate her. She is often willing and pliable. However, you must fulfill the role of leader, director, teacher and steward of the relationship. That is our God-given privilege and responsibility. Take joy and pleasure in drinking deeply from your cistern and no other.

"There is only one woman deserving of your love, the one God gave you and no other."

-Dr. David Scott
Pastor/Educator

Thoughts and Reflections

Areas of Improvement

1. _____

_____

_____

2. _____

_____

_____

3. _____

_____

_____

Prayer for Satisfaction

Gracious God, I pray that you would be merciful and kind. I ask that you help this man and make his eyes, heart, mind and focus remain steadily on the wife you have given him. In a world full of distractions and temptations, Lord, help him to stay satisfied and content with the one you have provided for him. Place blinders on his eyes. Fix his gaze in one direction. Make his longings, desires and thirst be quenched only from the well you have created and designed for him to draw. Make his passions burn for his wife and her alone. Give him the strength and courage to resist all temptations and carnality. Amen.

Tip #5

Honor God by loving your wife as she is, rejoicing over her. Let her be the source of your comfort and delight now and forever!

Proverbs 5:18 "Let your wife be a fountain of blessing for you. Rejoice in the wife of your youth."

To HAVE A wife is a beautiful thing. No matter the challenges, frustrations and moments of difficulty. The good days always outweigh the perceived bad days. As husbands, if we are honest and reflective, we will realize that where it counts most, our lives have improved and have become better because of the partners God has so graciously given us. In many instances, for the first time, we are free to be ourselves and not pretend to be the person we think we should. We no longer have to act and pretend because we have a wife, bride, partner and companion. God has provided and given us our source of satisfaction, joy and pleasure. We need not look any further. He has given us a mate, companion and partner to experience and explore everything we dare together with His divine blessing. God has blessed us tremendously. We no longer have to find or seek the arms of scandalous, immoral and promiscuous women. We have a fountain of comfort. We have been given a wife to turn to for support, perfectly fitted to meet our physical, emotional and spiritual needs.

God created Marriage. Realizing man's needs, longings and desires, he made the woman for him. As his greatest gift, she compliments him, adding significantly to his life. Without her, his life cannot reach the peak of fulfillment or completeness. We find the softness, gentleness, beauty, tenderness, empathy, compassion, warmth and peace we often lack and so desperately need in a wife. If we have been found worthy in the sight of God to receive the gift of a wife, let us find delight, comfort, pleasure and extreme joy in developing, cultivating and nurturing her into the partner we need for life's journey. Also, let us be intentional in becoming the man, leader, protector and companion that encourages her to become her best. We are created and intended to be each other's support.

Marriage is not a sprint, but a long and continuous marathon. In a wife, God has given us a teammate and partner to walk, jog, sprint and run with for a lifetime. If we fulfill our role and responsibility as a husband, she will journey with us through the ups and downs, highs and lows, light and dark, to the hilltops and low valleys. A wife will stand and sit; she will be there when the years are good, bad and both. Unlike any other, a wife will be there when we lose the youthful bounce in our step, our stomachs' flatness and when the hairs' color fades from dark to peppered, then gray. In his perfect will, God created two from one and intended for the two to rejoin in Marriage as one. There is nothing more precious, loyal and faithful as a good and godly wife. She is a treasure. If God has so graciously blessed us with a wife, we should rejoice, be glad and praise Him, recognizing her for all she is, has been and will become for us throughout the years.

As time passes, nothing stays the same. We get older, our bodies change, we look different and so do our spouses. All of these things are a part of the natural progression of life. Changes in physical aesthetics and appearance can never negate a wife's worth, value and benefit over the years. With the passing of time, as we assess the things that remain and have been constant, we should praise God for a faithful partner. Friends and acquaintances often come and go. Family members become estranged and abandon. Children grow up, get married, move away and start families of their own. However, if we follow the example of Christ, love and cherish our wives sacrificially, she will be the source and continuous comfort of our lives until death. Let us rejoice in the wife that stands with us; rejoice in her and regard her as a precious treasure given to us by a loving and compassionate Father, God.

"Marriage is a daily commitment and choice to love the partner you have been blessed with, realizing that in them is all that you need."

-Dr. David Scott
Pastor/Educator

Thoughts and Reflections

Areas of Improvement

1. _____

_____

_____

2. _____

_____

_____

3. _____

_____

_____

Prayer for Joy and Delight

Great God, I pray you would help this man find overwhelming pleasure and delight in his precious bride. I ask he finds daily happiness and comfort in being at her side. I pray he rejoices all the days of their union together and acknowledges she is a blessing in his life. I pray he values her above all others and takes great joy in her being his reflection. In a world full of many variations and kinds of flowers, I pray he remains steadfast in confidence that he has received the most beautiful and fragrant in the field, Amen.

Tip #6

A wife is a treasure. She should never be mistreated or taken for granted. Love her, cherish her and thank God for His favor in your life!

Proverbs 18:22 "The man who finds a wife finds a treasure, and he receives favor from the LORD."

Although in many circles, it is considered an unimportant thing and in others, something to be dreaded and avoided, Marriage is a blessing from the Lord. It is a privilege to be married. God has declared it a good thing when we find a wife. We obtain His favor in our lives. We all need God's blessing. A wife is that blessing. Only a fool rejects and denies God's purpose for his life. God is clear in his declaration to withhold from those that seek him and love him nothing good. As a loving and gracious father, He always knows what is best for us.

The writer says when a man finds a wife, he finds something both useful and beneficial. When God blesses us to discover and come upon a woman with such qualities, characteristics and beauty that we want to make her a wife, we have found something priceless. All women do not necessarily possess the qualities necessary to be a good wife. Not all women are kind, gentle, loving, compassionate, unselfish, modest, respectful, peaceful, moral or committed to a life of pursuing God, his word and supporting their partner and family. No degree of outward or physical beauty can make up for the lack of these qualities. No marriage can last if built on either a man or a woman's temporal and fleeting physical beauty. There has to be more. The beauty of the heart, mind and soul is a far more enduring and lasting foundation.

No matter how beautiful outwardly, not all women are ready to be wives. Sadly, we live in a world that does not prepare them to be. Long gone are the days when girls are taught early by their wise and godly mothers, aunts and grandmothers the skills to create and build a happy home. Many believe those practices are irrelevant, outdated and old-fashioned. Society teaches girls and young women to care little about the inside and focus wholly on the exterior. Rarely is there mention of the heart, mind or soul. Although external beauty is essential to some degree, internal beauty is more critical. The woman that understands the benefit, significance and importance of cultivating her spiritual development, nurturing her character and continence and her relationship with God in preparation for the day her Boaz, finds her is a jewel. She is a rare treasure among fools-gold, a diamond among common stones, waiting for discovery.

When a man comes upon and discovers a wife, a woman of exceptional character and graciousness, indeed he has found a good thing. If God, in His kindness, has granted us the privilege to find a wife, we should value, love, respect and treasure her as a gift. In her, God has blessed us with a gift that will support us, help us, pray for us and encourage us in all situations. Finding a wife is truly a demonstration of God's grace and favor.

"There is tremendous joy and satisfaction found in Marriage. It is God's special creation, gift and plan for a man and woman's celebration of each other."

-Dr. David Scott
Pastor/Educator

Thoughts and Reflections

Areas of Improvement

1. _____

_____

_____

2. _____

_____

_____

3. _____

_____

_____

Prayer for Wisdom and Appreciation

Dear Lord, I pray that you help this man appreciate the perfect gift you have given him. Through your divine wisdom, help him understand she is a treasure and prize of the highest value. God, I pray that you teach, guide and give him the capacity and words to comfort and encourage her, as it is a husband's obligation and responsibility. Father, I pray you would strengthen and guide him in the way he treats, provides and cares for her. Help him O God to value his work, privilege and role as a husband. Help him to see his wife as more than a woman, object or trophy. Let him know the strength in her weaknesses, peace in her calmness and empowerment in her smile. Let him see her as a compliment and welcomed addition to his life, allowing him the wisdom to surrender, be open and vulnerable and receptive to all she can offer as a partner and friend. Amen.

Tip #7

When God blesses a man to find a wife, we have discovered a priceless jewel. She should be prized, respected and shown her worth!

Proverbs 31:10 "Who can find a virtuous and capable wife? She is more precious than rubies."

IN A WORLD full of pretenders, wannabes, imitators and so-called influencers, what are men to do? Everywhere we look, girls and women of all ages leave nothing to the imagination. Everything is exposed. As the days pass, morals, integrity and character are becoming increasingly loose. Far too many women and lovers are available and willing for the right price. The majority are like puppies in the display window, dancing and performing tricks for attention. I can hear the song playing in my mind with the all too familiar lyrics, "How much is that doggie in the window? The one with the waggly tail. How much is that doggie in the window? I do hope that doggie's for sale." For fame, money and attention, all can be seen, and much more can be had.

The ability to find a godly wife and not just someone to marry is no small task. Many women express the idea and desire to be married, but have no concept of what Marriage entails and demands. However, in all honesty, there are no fewer men in that same position. As men, we should work diligently to be husbands to our wives, particularly when we are confident God has smiled on us and blessed us with the gift we have received. The scriptures asked the question, who can find an excellent wife? It goes on to inform us that this kind of wife is more precious than jewels. She is more valuable than a precious treasure of diamonds, pearls, rubies and emeralds. What makes her so lovely is that she shines in comparison to others. She stands apart, not because of external characteristics but because of what she possesses on the inside. These qualities are undeniable and recognized by all. She is a beacon to all around her, admired and welcomed among her friends and peers.

When God has blessed us to have a wife that takes delight and pleasure in serving us as the husband and priest in our home, we must recognize we are highly favored. An excellent wife is one that enjoys cooking, cleaning, serving and caring for her family. She delights and takes her identity not from the outside world's standards, but the implications of her duty and role as a wife, companion, and helper of her partner and nurturer of her family. An excellent wife does not need to fight with her partner about money, leadership, responsibility or her need for independence. She is comfortable allowing her partner to lead, provide and function in his role without contention or disagreement. She understands her role and function as a support and partner. She understands and welcomes her role as a companion. She works diligently to do her part, adding and increasing the wealth and resources of her home. It is her ambition to care for her family and meet their needs in every way. She is a delight to her husband.

"There is nothing more radiant than the glow of a woman basking in the knowledge that she is valued, esteemed and prized for her inner and outward magnificence and beauty."

-Dr. David Scott
Pastor/Educator

Thoughts and Reflections

Areas of Improvement

1. _____

_____

_____

2. _____

_____

_____

3. _____

_____

_____

Prayer for Understanding

Father, I pray that you move on the mind and heart of this man. I pray that you speak to him and whisper into the depth and recesses of his soul. God, I pray that you press on him the importance of his mate and the companion you have given and the splendor of the future you destined them to share. Help him to recognize that a wife is a treasure to be prized, valued and esteemed. God, help him to know that you have given him a rare find, something many desire, but few experience in this life. You have found him worthy of being a husband. Teach him what it means, and give him understanding and wisdom of the fact he has received a helper, capable companion, supporter and co-builder of his dreams, Amen.

Tip #8

God has given you a wife. She is yours to care for, protect and nurture. Decide and commit never to let outside influences separate you. She belongs to you and you alone!

Mark 10:8-9 "Since they are no longer two but one, let no one split apart what God has joined together."

Marriage is one of the most challenging and trying relationships we can ever be a part of. No matter how much we love our partners and they love us, there will be difficult moments, times and seasons. There will be days when it seems all forms of support and foundation have fallen. Anyone who is married long enough can affirm there are moments when we question why, how and who encouraged our union. There are situations and scenarios when emotions betray, leading us to believe we may have made a marital choice mistake. However, we must remember that even though Marriage can stretch us to a breaking point, it is undeniably the most rewarding, significant and meaningful relationship we can ever enter, cultivate and learn from; all others pale in comparison.

Without exception, all marriages have challenges. Do not be fooled. Everything that glitters is not gold. All marriages have challenges. No standard of beauty, sexual chemistry or amount of money can insulate and shelter us from this certainty. It is only a matter of when, what kind and how big the challenges. There is no relationship between two people sharing life that does not go through pains, groaning and struggles. Challenges are a part of the marriage scenario; however, the challenges are not significant. What is most important is how we handle the hard times. Few pay much attention to the words repeated during the marriage ceremony. Anxious to get the formalities over and move to the honeymoon, quickly we mouth the terms of our covenant promise and vows worn before men, women, God and his angels. When challenges arise, we forget our commitment to the question asked, "Do you take this woman to be your wife, to have and to hold from this day forward, for better, for worse, for richer, for poorer, in sickness and in health, to love and to cherish, until death do you part?" We all respond in the affirmative, "I Do!" When we are angry, frustrated and hurt, we forget our vow. However, God does not forget.

When we get married, God desires that we uphold the promises and vows made. No matter what it takes, it is God's will that we maintain, safeguard and hold tight to our union. Though Marriage has challenges, it is our responsibility to allow nothing beyond death to separate us. We should never take our problems and disputes to family members, relatives or friends. However consulted, if they are unwilling to offer encouragement, support and possible resolution to mend the breach in our Marriage, their suggestions and advice are unwelcomed. Our relationship, happiness and loneliness are our own doing should we make the wrong choice. When God united and joined us to our wives, it was not for practice or trial basis. Scripture instructs us clearly, let nothing come between the union God has blessed and divinely joined together.

The choice and decision to abandon the wife God has given is a deliberate act of disobedience and rebellion against God and his plan for us. God desires that the marital union remain intact if reasonably possible. However, there are situations when this plan seems improbable, specifically when there is emotional, psychological, and physical abuse. In these scenarios help, counseling, and intervention is necessary. Initially, the only justifiable excuse and acceptable reason to end the marital union was adultery, the verifiable physical and sexual activity with another outside your marriage. Even then, God has given advisement to forgive and remain committed if the offender earnestly and sincerely asked your forgiveness. We can always choose to ignore and disregard. In Marriage, there will be innumerable opportunities. If the union is to remain healthy, forgiveness must be readily available. Both husband and wife must always be ready to forgive, just as God is ready to forgive all. That is the exchange, the give and take of Marriage.

We do not fall in or out of love, particularly with our spouses. Genuine and authentic love has nothing or very little to do with a feeling or emotion. Feelings and emotions change based on situations, circumstances and scenarios. Real love is a choice. Daily, we can and must choose to love our spouses. If any marriage is to last, survive, mature and grow into all it can be, the choice to love and forgive must be deliberate and intentional. The apostle Paul gives us a more precise definition of what real love looks like in action. In 1 Corinthians 13:4-7, He says, "Love is patient and kind. Love is not jealous or boastful or proud or rude. It does not demand its own way. It is not irritable, and it keeps no record of being wronged. It does not rejoice about injustice, but rejoices whenever the truth wins out. Love never gives up, never loses faith, is always hopeful, and endures through every circumstance."

"If God, the Maker and Creator of the most perfect unions joined you as one, nothing in heaven or earth can tear you apart. The two have become, and are one in every way."

-Dr. David Scott
Pastor/Educator

Thoughts and Reflections

Areas of Improvement

1. _____

_____

_____

2. _____

_____

_____

3. _____

_____

_____

Prayer for Commitment and Dedication

O Lord, you made man and woman perfect for each other. You created man from the red earth, magnificent in every way. However, recognizing it not good that man travel life alone, from him you designed a perfectly fitted and exceptional compliment, the woman. Father, it is your desire that they no longer dwell apart, but the two be forever joined as one. Lord, I pray that you help this man and his companion understand, commit and resolve to fulfill their roles and obligations to each other. I pray together they fight with vigor and all diligence to sustain their union and let nothing come between them. I pray that all powers of evil, division and divisiveness be broken, cast down and made void in their lives and union. I ask that you wrap your great, powerful and massive hand around them, keeping that which you have joined together safe from the works of darkness, Amen.

Tip #9

Resist sexual temptation outside your Marriage. Let your desires and passions burn only for your own wife and partner!

1 Corinthians 7:2 "Because there is so much sexual immorality, each man should have his own wife, and each woman should have her own husband."

THE WORLD IS filled with every conceivable temptation with the single objective of leading men and women as far as possible from the plan and perfect will of God for their lives. Satan is the Prince of this world and effectively uses his limited power to appeal to all men and women's ambitions, lust and secret desires. Though he is not a god, he has control over this present world, and he is capable of making so many things look incredibly attractive and desirable. His audacity and boldness know no bounds or limitations. Scriptures tell us that Lucifer even planned to tempt the King of Heaven, saying in Matthew 4:8-10, "The devil took Him to a very high mountain and showed Him all the kingdoms of the world and their glory. "All this I will give you," he said, "if you will fall down and worship me." "Away from me, Satan!" Jesus declared. "For it is written: Worship the Lord your God and serve Him only."

Satan is a great tempter. This is a clear and irrefutable fact. He appeals to the base and carnality of all men and women. Sex is everywhere. We cannot turn on the television, watch a movie, preview a video trailer or listen to popular music without being bombarded by the idea, suggestion and emphasis on sexuality and the act of engaging in sex with some new, random and attractive stranger. The hookup and casual dating culture have exploded. The ancient writers prophesied that the world would advance in both wisdom and wickedness. Justifying themselves in their own eyes, most people abandon the moral and righteous law and commands of God to do what seems right, logical and feels good. The list of new and popular dating apps is staggering and growing daily. Casual and uncommitted sexual encounters are made increasingly acceptable and easy, thanks to dating apps like Our Time, Bumble, Plenty of Fish, Hinge, Hung, OKCupid, Zoosk, eHarmony, Tinder, Her, Happn, The Inner Circle, Coffee Meet Bagel and Pickable to name a few.

As men, God has commanded us to stand and be the priest of our homes and the moral and righteous leaders of our families. This is an ancient and unchanging mandate. Since the days of the apostles, the lust of men and women's hearts have led them away from God's perfect plan and will for their lives. The truth of that reality has increased and intensified with passing and technologically progressive years. Presently, the world has no genuine and authentic modesty or discretion. According to statistics, 200,000 Americans are classified as porn addicts, and no less than 40 million American people regularly visit porn sites. Men and women have wrongly chosen to do what is right in their own eyes. God is not pleased, because people all over the world are freely and willingly engaging in lifestyles and sexual practices against God's law; men and women should marry because they are incapable of controlling their sexual appetites and desires. Men and women should have their own mates to satisfy their needs, and experience the fullness and benefit of union. For both the man and women, marriage allows both partners to growth emotionally and personally. Marriage fosters and promotes mental and physical health, and contributes significantly to longevity.

Tip #9

Marriage produces many of life's happiest moments, and provides an overwhelming since of life satisfaction, direction, and overall purpose.

God's perfect will is that men and women experience the best and fullness that can be discovered between a man and woman. However, those discoveries are meant to be explored in the legal bonds of holy matrimony. There is no joy, peace or blessing to be gained or experienced in violation and rebellion of the law and instruction of the great Creator. God created both Marriage and sex. They are not exclusive of each other. They were created to be experienced and enjoyed together. The attempt to enjoy and find pleasure from the act created for couples joined in Marriage without the commitment, obligation and responsibility is an attempt at theft. It is an attempt to circumvent the matchless and inconceivable plan of God for our own. It consistently brings pain, sadness and regret. Sex outside of marriage damages and destroys what God divinely purposed. It has been confirmed that pornography-use increases the marital infidelity rate by more than 300%. Sex outside of Marriage is a gross, distorted and perverted forgery of God's authentic masterpiece.

There is absolutely nothing wrong with sex or the desire to have sex. God created sex to be fully enjoyed. However, it is meant to be enjoyed with our wives. We hear the words of the apostle addressing an issue of sexuality in light of Christ's soon return, saying in 1Corinthians 7:2-4, "Yes, it is good to abstain from sexual relations. But because there is so much sexual immorality, each man should have his own wife, and each woman should have her own husband. The husband should fulfill his wife's sexual needs, and the wife should fulfill her husband's needs. The wife gives authority over her body to her husband, and the husband gives authority over his body to his wife."

In the bonds of Marriage, sex brings no embarrassment, shame or sadness. A husband and wife are free to exercise their sexual rights without violation of the other's wishes. Between married couples, the only limitation is imagination. God desires husbands and wives to enjoy each other fully and completely. Each partner has a divine obligation and responsibility to the other. There are no acceptable excuses for violation of the covenant vow of Marriage. The scriptures tell us in Hebrews 13:4 "Marriage should be honored by all, and the marriage bed kept pure, for God will judge the adulterer and all the sexually immoral."

"Being faithful and loyal to the partner God gave you is not a suggestion or an option. It is an obligation, responsibility and duty."

-Dr. David Scott
Pastor/Educator

Thoughts and Reflections

Areas of Improvement

1. _____

   _____

   _____

2. _____

   _____

   _____

3. _____

   _____

   _____

Prayer for Resistance and Strength

Lord, I pray that you help this man and woman as they strive with all-purpose, desire and conviction to live out together the life you planned and wish for them as husband and wife. God, I ask you to endow them with divine and supernatural strength, tenacity and determination to withstand every temptation and live righteously in union and marital fellowship. Father, I ask that you lift them high above every spirit, thought, desire and imagination that opposes your perfect plan and will for their lives and Marriage. Great God, I ask that you help them shine as lights in the darkness and serve as examples of what can be when you are the center, focus and final authority on the way and direction they should take in every situation and circumstance. Help them, O Lord, to stand like trees planted by rivers of cool and refreshing waters, unwavering, unfaltering and unyielding because of the depths of their roots in you and the truth of your perfect word. Lord, I ask that when the powers of darkness work to oppose your will for their lives and union that you raise a warrior's shield against every attack and weapon, Amen.

Tip #10

Love your wife with all within you. No sacrifice is too big to make in a demonstration of love for your bride!

Ephesians 5:25 "Husbands, love your wives, as Christ loved the church and gave himself up for her."

When we are happy, and in our relationship's honeymoon phase, we feel satisfied and head over heels with our partners. However, this feeling and emotion tend to wane and decrease over time. Some situations and circumstances arise in a marriage that cause things we say to contradict our actions and how we treat our spouses, thus, falling significantly beneath love's definition. In the mind and sight of God, no instability in our commitment is acceptable. Following Christ's example, nothing can separate from the love of God. Even when we are unlovable, disobedient and rebellious, God is gracious and kind. When we abandon Him, He remains faithful. Reflecting on the prodigal son's story and image, and the father ever watchful, waiting and vigilant, God never gives upon us. His love for us is unwavering. We can always return.

God's call and demand to love our wives are more significant than any other relational obligation. It is greater than any other in our lives. We can love family members and relatives; however, love for our wives must surpass even that because God has joined us as one. God does not suggest. He commands us to love our partner. He tells us we have an obligation and responsibility not just to like them when they: are most lovable, do what we want, behave as we wish and fulfill our desires. We are expected and demanded to love them genuinely, authentically and unconditionally. Not only are we told to love them, but He also gives clear and specific instructions. He tells us to love them, like the Lord and Savior, Jesus Christ loves his bride, the Church. Following his example, we are expected to give our lives for her benefit. As our life partner and companion, we should be willing to die daily to preserve the one we love. Christ loved his bride so much; in a demonstration, he died on a rugged cross on a hill called Calvary in Jerusalem.

Love is not what we say, but what we do. There is no greater extraordinary demonstration of love than a willingness to sacrifice. God tells us to love our wives the same way he loves his bride. He was willing to give himself wholly and entirely. What could 'greater love' be than the one Christ demonstrated? He gave us this demonstration as the highest example of what love looks like in action. Christ shows that nothing is too much to offer and sacrifice for our spouses, not even our lives from the model presented. When we take on a wife, we forfeit the luxury of living selfishly. The day we say those familiar and sobering words "I DO," our lives are no longer our own. We have chosen a life of sacrifice and self-denial.

If we profess to love our wives, no sacrifice is too great. It should not be difficult to bring her flowers, candy or things she likes and treat her with the highest degree of respect. After making the promise and vow to cherish her, a wife is no longer a random and unfamiliar stranger. She is a friend, companion, confidante, partner, supporter and helpmate. She should be valued and recognized as a treasure. We demonstrate our love through words and deeds. Not only do we offer lip service, we put our money where our mouth is. We put action behind our words. We practice what we have been preaching. God demands that we consistently prove our love through action. Because we love them, it should not be challenging to help them when they need us. We must learn to find contentment and satisfaction in being needed and relied upon. We must learn to be gracious and willing to serve in the big and small things asked of us, even when we do not necessarily feel up to it or in the mood.

Love is not always convenient. Real love costs. The cost is what makes love so desirable. Men and women all over the world desperately seek to find, embrace and experience genuine love at least once, even if only for a moment, briefly. A writer once said, "It is better to have loved and lost than never to have loved at all." If God has blessed and given us a partner to love and cherish, there should be nothing we are unwilling to do in demonstration and proof. We have an obligation and responsibility to protect and guard the heart, mind and spirit of the wives God has entrusted to us. God calls us to be her covering and protector. No act, deed or service is too great. As husbands, we should begin daily with commitment and sacrifice. If our goal and objective are to emulate our Savior's example, we must be ready and willing to give our all, just as he did for his bride, the Church and us.

"The cost of a good, strong and lasting marriage is sacrifice. The more beautiful the Marriage, the greater the commitment and willingness to sacrifice on the part of those united."

-Dr. David Scott
Pastor/Educator

Thoughts and Reflections

Areas of Improvement

1. _____

_____

_____

2. _____

_____

_____

3. _____

_____

_____

Prayer for Humility and Sacrifice

God, I pray that you do what only you can do as the Creator of all things. Lord, I ask that you move on the heart of this man, making him a vessel fit for the task of serving as a selfless protector, caretaker and provider for the companion you have given him in the form of a wife. Father, I pray that you create in him the ability to be compassionate, selfless and willing to place her needs above his own. Father, help him be gentle with his words, make still his tongue when the cost is too great and show him there is greater strength and compassion in his silence. O God, please help him realize that his happiness, contentment and joy are wrapped and comingled with hers. Let him see his wife's laughter, smile and peace as the product of his willingness to make her feel valued, prized and highly desired. Show him, O God, how his every sacrifice will return immeasurable reward. Let his desire to sacrifice grow in intentionality, frequency and sincerity each day. Father, teach, show and help him to see his every sacrifice as an acceptable and reasonable act of service for his beloved, Amen.

Tip #11

Love your wife no differently than you love yourself. Care for her unselfishly!

Ephesians 5:28-29 "Husbands ought to love their wives as they love their own bodies. For a man who loves his wife shows love for himself. No one hates his own body, but feeds and cares for it, just as Christ cares for the Church."

WHEN SAYING WE love our wives, are we sure we understand the depth, strength and magnitude of what is required of us as husbands? Far too often, we are not. We say it, and to some significant degree, we mean it. However, what God demands of us is more. The love we are to render and share with our partners is one of completeness, wholeness and without restraint. As husbands, we are to love our wives without limitations and conditions.

When God tells us to love our wives, he means sincerely and authentically. God challenges us to examine and consider the love, regard and care we take for ourselves and make the comparison. There is no mistake; we love ourselves. It shows in our grooming, the clothes we choose and buy to wear, the haircuts and styles we get, our choice of jewelry and the energies we exert to keep ourselves physically fit and appealing. Everyone around us can see that we love ourselves by the physical, tangible and clear examples and demonstrations of personal self-care. Is that same evidence apparent regarding our wives? Can others see the cultivation, development and adornment of our wives both outwardly and internally? Do we give her a constant and continuous reason to smile, be joyous and pleasant?

Just as the love demonstrated for ourselves is evident, so should it be for our wives. God wants us to love our spouses no less than we love ourselves. We are to be no less selfish with them than we are with ourselves. If we deny ourselves nothing, we should neither deny them anything. God has united us as one with them. To look upon them should be as gazing in a mirror. They are a clear reflection of our love, care and consideration. Because we do our best to safeguard our own needs, we should also ensure she likewise lacks nothing. A wife's neglect and lack are a reflection of the husband. It is the husband's responsibility and obligation to care for the wife in every area. As protectors and guardians, husbands are required to make the wife secure and cared for in every place, even areas she might be unaware. As a husband, our job and responsibility are to cultivate and make her the very best she can be, no matter the sacrifice.

By loving our wives as we do our bodies, we intentionally deny them nothing. In doing so, we prove ourselves wise, recognizing she belongs to us. We confirm our understanding that nobody ever logically hated and abused his own body. On the contrary, wisely, everything is done to care for and preserve the body. In the same way, a prudent man cares for and keeps his wife. In the same way, he cares for his own body, providing every conceivable resource and nourishment; husbands are responsible for ensuring their bride's well-being, as Christ does for us.

"When a man views and sees his wife as a reflection, he recognizes his privilege and obligation to treat her as an extension of himself."

-Dr. David Scott
Pastor/Educator

Thoughts and Reflections

Areas of Improvement

1. _____

_____

_____

2. _____

_____

_____

3. _____

_____

_____

Prayer for Selflessness

Father, I pray you would help this man embrace the attitude, mentality and commitment to selflessness. God, I pray you to endow him with the spirit of selflessness, teaching him that he and the wife you have provided are one. I ask Lord that you teach him your perfect way. Reveal the beauty and privilege of the charge you have entrusted to him and that his wife is a reflection of himself. Help him understand that his wife is a benefit and not a burden. Breathe on him; fill him with your gentle and tender spirit, making it easy for him to give of himself for her benefit. Help him understand that he cannot profess love if he is unwilling to provide all of himself for her, just as you did for your bride, Amen.

Tip #12

Love your wife with such passion, conviction and sincerity that your devotion commands the respect you deserve!

Ephesians 5:33 "Each man must love his wife as he loves himself, and the wife must respect her husband."

God requires us to love our wives as ourselves. There are no excuses or exceptions. We should shower them with the love they are entitled to and deserve. Wives deserve the same commitment, conviction and intensity that we allow ourselves. She deserves our very best. Selected and chosen from among millions to join us on life's journey, why should she not be cherished and treated like a most valuable treasure? As husbands, we receive the privilege to be protectors, providers and nurturers. God has given us someone to care for and to care for us.

How we show our love is critical. Often, we get frustrated feeling our intentions and efforts may be unappreciated, even when we give our best. However, there is a solution. To better understand how our gestures can be best received, we must ask our partner questions and not assume that our efforts, no matter how sincere, meet their expectations and needs. The most effective way of demonstrating love to our partner is by discovering their specific and unique love language. No two people are the same, nor do they necessarily share the same vocabulary. Each person has a language of love. Many marital struggles are the result of failure to identify our partner's love language. There are no less than five known love languages, namely touch, gifts, affection, acts of service and quality time. Failure to identify the language required to convey "I love you" to our partner and vice versa can be disastrous.

Most women love when we make them feel prioritized, significant and valuable. For women, this is a universal reality. Whenever and however we accomplish this, we show and demonstrate we love them. We win whenever we can achieve this. Women are more likely to experience love through acts of service, words of affirmation, as well as gifts. However, men receive love differently. Men often feel most loved by the woman in their life through her hugs, kisses, affectionate smiles, demonstration of gratitude, and intentional praise. Specifically, men tend to feel most loved when they recognize that their manhood is valued and appreciated. Respect is a very important piece of how men experience love. It is our partner's responsibility to make us feel valued and respected in a demonstration of love. Nevertheless, we should treat them well, encouraging and motivating them to render to us the respect warranted and desired. We have no right to demand respect. Instead, we should live and love our partners in ways that earn their respect and appreciation.

"Married couples are given the opportunity and responsibility to love each other with abandon, and practice the art and game of out loving and caring for each other daily for a life time in every way possible."

-Dr. David Scott
Pastor/Educator

Thoughts and Reflections

Areas of Improvement

1. _____

_____

_____

2. _____

_____

_____

3. _____

_____

_____

Prayer for Submission and Honor

Great and Eternal God, I pray that you would guide, lead and direct this man and woman in every interaction they share. Let both of them see the other as the vessel you have chosen to enrich their shared lives together. Help this man value his wife as he values himself, and this bride to extend the love and respect due to the husband she cherishes. Make them pliable, willing and capable of serving each other. Father, make what they desire for themselves also a desire for the other. Let their love and commitment toward each other become unshakable, unwavering and relentless. Help them to join and unite as one in every way, valuing the other more with each passing day, striving with patience and perseverance to grow deeper in the love they profess for each other as husband and wife, Amen.

Tip #13

Treat your wife with respect. Practice the intentionality of gentleness as a demonstration of love!

Colossians 3:19 "Husbands, love your wives and never treat them harshly."

As husbands, God has commanded us to love our wives. However, we are required to do more than pay the bills, keep the lights on and re-stock food in the refrigerator, cabinets and on the table. It is far too easy for us to conclude that if we are working hard, coming home every day, not hanging out with our friends all times of the night, not cheating not spending the majority of our free time playing video games, watching porn or passed out drunk, then we are good husbands. Suppose we are doing our best to ensure our partner has what we perceive nothing to complain about because she does not have to work, has a car to drive, money in her bank account, access to ours and the luxury to do with her time as she chooses. In that case, we believe we deserve a celebration for our acts and demonstration of love.

Although those things are great and commendable, they are the kind of things we should do as husbands, protectors, providers and men that genuinely value the treasure and gift God has so graciously given us. Providing for our spouses' financial needs, wants and desires requires little effort and sacrifice on our part. Many husbands have money to burn. For these husbands, it requires no real effort to purchase luxury homes, cars, boats, land, designer handbags, shoes or clothes. However, he may be lacking in giving his time, affection, service and affirming words. She may never fully perceive how much she is genuinely loved if her husband never conveys his love in her unique love language. A million-dollar home, car or yacht does not say "I Love You" more clearly than a quiet, intimate and relaxed day of talking, sharing and togetherness if her love language is "quality time."

Women are not easily understood. As men, we rarely know their expectations, as well as the things they want or what and when to say. That is just the nature of women. A plethora of books have been written on the subject surrounding the differences between men and women. One author's attempt to explain the differences, titled a book *Men Are from Mars, Women Are from Venus*. Because of the differences between men and women, we cannot treat our spouses how we do our friends, particularly our male friends. We cannot talk to them any way we wish, no matter the circumstance. Even when we are angry, frustrated and tired, we must be mindful of how we address them. We cannot forget that our wife is a treasure. Gold is still gold, even when it is tarnished and unpolished. Even when gold is unrefined and less aesthetically appealing, it does not lose its worth. It is always valuable.

Besides loving our wives by caring for them and meeting their physical and tangible needs, God instructs us to deal with them gently and not harshly. She is designated the weaker of the two in the relationship, not the lesser. Our spouses are frequently in need of our help, encouragement, support and assurance. When she is disagreeable and stubborn, the decision to mistreat, demean and tear her down will never improve the situation. However, listening, being kind, considerate and seeking to understand how to meet her emotional needs and make her feel loved, valued and wanted will. When she is acting unlovable and is still treated with

Tip #13

love, value and respect as our treasure, we make deposits in our marital bank that will yield immeasurable returns. There is always an underlying issue. It might serve us well to discover what it is and work hard to find a solution.

"Disagreements and misunderstandings are inevitable in Marriage. However, gentleness, tenderness and soft words bring quick end to most quarrels. A kind word and a listening ear are vital and crucial characteristics a loving husband must have."

-Dr. David Scott
Pastor/Educator

Thoughts and Reflections

Areas of Improvement

1. _____

_____

_____

2. _____

_____

_____

3. _____

_____

_____

Prayer for Patience and Gentleness

Father, it is you who designed the institution of Marriage knowing best for men and women. Lord, I pray that you would grant this husband the patience and tenderness necessary to build his wife, nurturing her to become all she is capable of becoming. I pray that he daily grows in his ability as a builder and never a dismantler of her dreams, emotions or spirit. Lord, I pray his words are kind, gentle and considerate. Please help him to be long in gentleness and limited in his ability to hold grudges when he feels he has been slighted or wronged. I pray the love for his bride has no boundaries, and his willingness to sacrifice has no end. Great God, help him choose his words ever so wisely, and may his responses always be measured. Amen.

Tip #14

Communication is vital to a successful and enduring marriage. Show your wife you love her through acts of greater understanding!

1 Peter 3:7 "You husbands must give honor to your wives. Treat your wife with understanding as you live together. She may be weaker than you are, but she is your equal partner in God's gift of new life. Treat her as you should so your prayers will not be hindered."

WHEN A MAN loves his wife, not only does he demonstrate it by providing for her needs. He also does his best with intentionality to live with her pleasantly, soberly and in peace. A sure way to establish, restore and maintain stability in the home is to work toward clear and effective communication. Understanding is both essential and critical in any relationship. Marriage partners must be able to understand each other. When there is a breakdown in understanding and communication, the Marriage will inevitably have challenges and difficulties.

Peace in Marriage begins with good communication. Nothing impacts a relationship like poor communication. However, nothing mends, secures and strengthens a marital relation like effective communication. Not only do the scriptures remind us that the power of both life and death are in the tongue, but we are also told in Proverbs 15:1, "A gentle answer deflects anger, but harsh words make tempers flare." Far too often is the importance of communication overlooked, rarely considered or taken seriously. In Marriage, this is a mistake. Communication is the vehicle through which all aspects of the day-to-day functions of Marriage are performed and accomplished. When we cannot communicate and understand each other, we are incapable of creating the most fulfilling Marriage God intended.

Although communicating our needs, desires and fears can be challenging, for women, this can be significantly challenging. Still, we as husbands must be intentional and deliberate in communicating and making her secret thoughts, insecurities, desires and fears of speaking up and being vulnerable easy. Good communication makes much of the marriage experience smoother. If we communicate honestly, openly and unselfishly, our marital relationships have a significant possibility of growing and developing into something joyous, healthy and admirably happy. Open communication between husband and wife is the cornerstone of any long, lasting and fruitful union. Love, honesty, trust, respect and all other vital characteristics of a healthy marriage are not necessarily meaningful in and of themselves. However, communicating how we feel about our spouses helps struggling, mediocre and even good marriages transition, becoming exceptional and outstanding.

Scripture describes the woman as the weaker vessel. This description in no way negates her abilities, talents or strengths; on the contrary, it only speaks to her softer, gentler and innately sensitive character compared to the man. Men often identify and correlate love with respect. Women tend to associate and connect love with how we make them feel. Nothing makes a woman feel more loved than when we intentionally take time to listen to her concerns, show enthusiasm for her interests and do all we can to better understand her as a person and partner. Effective communication in Marriage is imperative. We must communicate openly and honestly about the things we love, appreciate and enjoy about our partner. However, it is equally important to share dislikes. Understanding acquired through effective communication is the foundation of a happy marriage.

In a demonstration of kindness, God has granted us a partner to walk with through the experience of life. A wife must be viewed and valued as a partner and co-regent. In the sight of God, husband and wife are a packaged deal, two for one. God does not support discord, conflict and contention, rejecting self-gratifying prayers. When we go before him, we must forgive and ask for forgiveness when necessary from the partner God has given us so that what we ask of him might be received according to his will. We never want our prayers hindered because we are not treating our spouses well. Sometimes, it is in the area of communication and understanding we fail the most. However, we are capable of doing better. God demands and requires it, giving us Christ's example as our model. No sacrifice is too great, even death.

"There are no perfect situations or circumstances, only what we do to make them the best they can be. Husbands should treat their wives as if God is watching, remembering their union should mirror his relationship with his bride."

-Dr. David Scott
Pastor/Educator

Thoughts and Reflections

Areas of Improvement

1. _____

_____

_____

2. _____

_____

_____

3. _____

_____

_____

Prayer for Understanding

Father, no matter the trial, issue or circumstance, I ask that you help this husband show kindness and compassion to this woman chosen to be his wife. God, create in him the ability to be vulnerable, open and selfless. Help him to become all his wife needs him to be, reflecting you in care and concern for his bride. Teach him, O Lord, to be understanding and receptive to the needs of his spouse. Show him the power of his tenderness and the strength of your grace. Teach him to see the beauty in his bride's softness and let her find immeasurable comfort in his embrace. I pray he will always be available and attentive to her voice, accommodate her needs and respond gently to her tears, Amen.

Final Thoughts

MARRIAGE IS A beautiful thing, created and designed by the great and matchless God of the universe. He made this great institution to be experienced, enjoyed and lived out between man and woman, his crowned treasures of creation. He cared so much for the man he formed and fashioned in the garden that he gave him a companion unlike any other. From the beginning until this present time, God's will is that men and women find in their union the divine richness and beauty of fellowship.

If man had the smallest understanding of Marriage's significance, he would hold fast with all available to him to the partner God so graciously offers as a co-laborer and sojourner in life's journey. Marriage is precious to God. Marriage is a reflection of his love for his bride, which is the Church. In His grace, He offers man the privilege of serving as His emissary in demonstration of love for his bride. A husband has the right and choice to serve as the reflection of Christ as a lover, protector, provider, nurturer, supporter and unwavering companion and friend.

The Lord has challenged man in the role of husband to a place of honor and distinction. It is a role to be desired and not deliberately and purposely avoided. All men cannot, and should not enter into the arena to contend for the title of husband. The husband's task, duty and function are not for the faint of heart. It is for those that understand and earnestly desire to emulate the example of the Lord Jesus Christ. In following Christ's example, we too must resolve no price too great or sacrifice unacceptable in demonstration of our function of husband.

The role of the husband, though challenging, trying and demanding, is temporal. We only have this task for a short while. There is no such union in heaven. We surrender our role and duty as a husband when we receive the awaited prize of slumber and rest. Someday, no man will have the role and responsibilities anymore. In heaven, we will no longer be husbands. There, we will meet the supreme example we have earnestly attempted to follow. We will all see the perfect husband, Jesus, and we will unite with him as his bride. We are reminded of this reality as we read the words of the apostle John in Revelations 19:6-8,

> "I heard a sound like the roar of a great multitude, like the rushing of many waters, and like a mighty rumbling of thunder, crying out: "Hallelujah! For the Lord our God, the Almighty reigns. Let us rejoice and be glad and give Him the glory. For the Marriage of the Lamb as come, and His bride has made herself ready. She was given clothing of fine linen, bright and pure."For the fine linen, she wears are the righteous acts of the saints."

Marriage is a practice, practical application and the ultimate experience in humility, temperance, daily refinement and development. Through the experience of Marriage, men and women have the opportunity and privilege of growing, stretching and gaining greater reliance on God to create in them the right spirit, character, attributes and attitudes to meet his expectations of the divine reflection of eternity. Only through Him can we be what He has intended us to be. We are not our own. We are merely clay, and He is the Potter. We do well to surrender, allowing Him to shape us and make us daily more in his likeness. Only in this yielding will we find success, joy and contentment. Marriage is God's creation. Only by following His instructions will we experience it as intended. Marriage is neither a struggle nor drudgery, as many contend.

Marriage by design is the sweetest and most beautiful reflection of God's unfailing, untarnished and relentless love for His creation, man and woman. Repeated; Marriage is the ultimate, beautiful and precious gift to a man and woman. However, the commitment, conviction, diligence, tenacity, reverence and superiority of quality we create of our Marriage are the ultimate gift in return to our God.

Made in the USA
Middletown, DE
18 March 2024